THE BURHĀN

Arguments for a Necessary Being Inspired by Islamic Thought

Mohammed Hijab

SAPIENCE
PUBLISHING

Copyright © 2021

Sapience Publishing. *First Edition*, 2021.

www.sapienceinstitute.org

Book Design: *Ummah Grafiks*

CONTENTS

INTRODUCTION

According to the most recent data published by Pew Research Center, 90% of Americans believe in a higher power.[1] Although many other people in the UK and US no longer believe in a particular religion, only 5% are strident atheists in a manner which indicates acceptance of the arguments of the New Atheists.[2] Percentage-wise, this may not seem like much, but 5% is a significant proportion of the overall population. The fact that some people are rejecting faith in God would suggest that either they are unconvinced with the evidence for God's existence, or that arguments for God's existence have been demolished. Considering this, it may come as a surprise that Richard Dawkins – probably the West's most popular academic atheist – dedicates only two pages to refuting the design argument for God's existence and five to Aquinas's cosmological argument in the *God Delusion*. The fact that New Atheists seem to have not engaged with the analytic evidence of theists, combined with the fact that analytic philosophy dominates most western university settings,[3] gives theists a wide theoretical opening. They can reintroduce some of the most enduring natural theological arguments posited

[1] Pew Forum (2019). *In U.S., Decline of Christianity Continues at a Rapid Pace* [online] Pew Research Centre Available at:
https://www.pewforum.org/2019/10/17/in-u-s-decline-of Christianity-continues-at-rapid-pace/.
[2] Woodhead, L., & Catto, R. (2012). *Religion and Change in Modern Britain*. Taylor & Francis Group, p. 246.
[3] Searle, J. (2002) Contemporary philosophy in the United States. Blackwell, p. 1.

throughout history.

Many of the arguments I will present in this book, I have used in applied settings for over a decade. In this time, I have had deep and meaningful conversations with hundreds of atheists and agnostics particularly in the UK. I aim to give the reader a flavour of the type of interactions I have had with people from different cross-sections of society. I will reference my experience with two characters who I will make reference to throughout this book. These two characters are not actual subjects but are hypothetical people or fictitious amalgams of people I have met. Subject A, who I shall call Richard, is the ultra-sceptic friend. He is 21 years of age and an ex-Christian. He entered university to study physics and philosophy. After taking a course on 'theories of the self', Richard had an existential crisis and became an atheist. Richard is disagreeable, extraverted, and non-caring. Subject B, who I shall call Betty, is a quiet person. Unlike Richard, Betty is an introvert. Betty is agnostic. Spends most of her time by herself either in her room or in the library. When I speak to Betty, Betty takes time to listen to what I say before replying to me. Unlike Richard, Betty is less interested in provoking a reaction from people but more in sharing ideas. Betty comes across as highly docile and placid especially in public settings in which she has much social anxiety. Betty has had a troubled upbringing with sexual and physical abuse in her formative years. Throughout this book where relevant, I will use my experiences with Betty and Richard as case study examples to outline some of the real-life complexities one may face in apologetic interactions.

Much is at stake in the presentation of these arguments for God's existence. For many, the intellectual validity of theism is predicated on the soundness of these arguments, and the degree to which they can be clearly articulated. For theists to be truly effective they must be able to justify their beliefs from first principles. Since ancient times, rational arguments have been posited for God's existence. For instance, Aristotle employs proof for an unmoved mover in a way which is analogous to arguments for God's existence. In the Christian tradition, Augustine, Anselm, and Aquinas formulated serious and rational arguments for God's existence. Maimonides – perhaps the most celebrated scholar in Jewish history – wrote the *Guide for the Perplexed*, in which he made a systematic case for God's existence using discursive reasoning. In the Islamic world, Ibn Sīnā (Avicenna), al-Ghazālī (Algazel), Ibn Rushd (Averroes), and many others contributed to this discourse by offering their own sets of proofs for God's existence. In a similar fashion, enlightenment and post-enlightenment philosophers including polymaths such as Gottfried Leibniz and Kurt Gödel presented new arguments as well. These and similar arguments have entered the academic debates that concern a sub-branch of philosophy known as 'Philosophy of Religion'. In this field, particular focus has been placed on both ontological arguments and cosmological arguments for God's existence. To be clear, when referring to ontological arguments I mean "a proof which argues for the existence of God entirely from *a priori* premises and makes no use of any premises that derive from our observation of the world".[4] On the other hand cosmological arguments are those which make direct reference to the cosmos in the premises.

In this book, I aim to specifically analyse Ibn Sīnā's *Burhān* argument for the existence of God, as I regard it as being most invulnerable to any type of counterattack. The *Burhān* argument postulates that a world with only contingent existences is inconceivable, as a contingent existence cannot

---

[4] Shihadeh, A. (2008). The existence of God. In Tim Winter (Ed.), *The Cambridge Companion to Classical Islamic Theology*. Cambridge University Press, p. 212.

cause itself. A set of an infinite number of contingent existences cannot explain the existence of all contingent existences, or else it would belong in another set, namely the set of necessary existence(s). As a necessary existence it would be an uncaused cause, and it could not be any other way. In short, Ibn Sīnā argues that the only way to explain the existence of anything is to postulate the existence of an uncaused cause, or a *wājib al-wujūd* ('necessary existence'). However, despite its impact, the *Burhān* has not been packaged for apologetic use for a modern audience. Accordingly, my novel contribution to the discourse surrounding God's existence is found in the intention of re-articulating this argument for theists attempting to make the case for religion to atheist audiences.

To this end, I will start this book with some translations of analytically important extracts from the work of Ibn Sīnā (some of which have hitherto not been translated from Arabic to English). I will then assess the reception of Ibn Sīnā's *Burhān* argument in the medieval world of both Christians and Muslims. Thereafter, I will present some modern usages of the cosmological and ontological arguments, while comparing them with the *Burhān*. I will then articulate my own proofs for the necessary existence of God, using the *Burhān* as my guide. In this, I will compose arguments informed by non-causal contingency and dependency which aim to circumnavigate some of the stock objections on causation and composition. In addition, I will answer some of the most prominent objections towards this argument, with the goal being to demonstrate how useful the *Burhān* argument can be in discussions between theists and atheists. To achieve this goal, I will bring in conversations with Richard and Betty, wherever possible.

4

Chapter 1
IBN SĪNĀ'S ARGUMENTS

Ibn Sīnā presents his arguments for God's existence in a number of his writings, mainly in Metaphysics *of the Cure (Al-Ilāhiyāt al-Shifā')*, *The Deliverance (Al-Najāh)*, and *The Pointers and Reminders (Al-Ishārāt wa al-tanbīhāt)*. These works address many other topics as well, like logic, mathematics, and natural philosophy. Ibn Sīnā employs a range of different arguments in these writings: some of which argue for God's existence from motion (inspired by Aristotle), others from causation, and even others from composition (which is an important corollary to arguments appealing to causation). In this chapter, I will briefly outline Ibn Sīnā's arguments from these sources, referring to both the relevance and function of his arguments in relation to contemporary debates between atheists and theists. The aim of Chapters 1 and 2 is to demonstrate why this particular rendition of the argument is particularly valuable in these debates. The intention is to provide theists intellectual ammunition that is currently either under-developed or completely lacking in both academic literature found in Philosophy of Religion publications and the most famous public engagements between theists and atheists in the last century.

When reading Ibn Sīnā, one must keep in mind that he often switches from informative to persuasive writing. Accordingly, one must be careful not to conflate Ibn Sīnā's logical and metaphysical taxonomies (which are intended as matter-of-fact clarifications) and his formal arguments. As an

5

example, the 6th chapter of Ibn Sīnā's *Metaphysics of the Cure* has been misunderstood to be an argument, where Ibn Sīnā's intention was most probably simply taxonomical. On this point, Daniel De Haan states:

> ...Avicenna's analysis of necessary and possible existence in Ilāhiyyāt I.6–7 could not be a formal demonstration for God's existence since these chapters are oriented towards providing us with insights into the proper first principles of metaphysics.[5]

Other scholars of Ibn Sīnā, such as Fazlur Rahman[6] and Parvis Morewedge[7] regard this kind of classification as an argument in and of itself.[8]

In what is perhaps the most comprehensive, yet concise passage written by the Persian philosopher demonstrating God's existence, we find Ibn Sīnā state in *The Deliverance*:

> There is no doubt that there is existence. Everything that exists is either contingent or necessary. If it is necessary, then the pursuit of the necessary existence is complete. If it is contingent, I will make clear that this contingent existence will ultimately return back to a necessary existence. Before this, I will present premises (to prove this thesis). Among these premises is [the assertion] that it is impossible for an infinite regress of causes to account for a

[5] De Haan, D. (2016). Where does Avicenna demonstrate the existence of God? *Arabic Sciences and Philosophy, 26*(1), p. 104.

[6] Rahman, F. (1963). Ibn Sina. In M.M. Sharif (Ed.), *A History of Muslim Philosophy,* pp. 480-506.

[7] Morewedge, P. (1979). *Islamic Philosophical Theology.* Suny Press, pp. 234-350.

[8] Both Morewedge and Rahman regard the argument as ontological.

contingent existence. That is because all contingent existences either all exist at once or do not exist at once. If they do not all exist at once and they are infinite, one preceding another, we will deal with this matter in another section of this book. If they are all together and there is no necessary existence in the set, [we find that] upon exhaustive analysis [and whether or not it is finite or infinite] the set [of contingent things] can either be composed of contingent things or necessary things. If, in the set, there is a necessary existence and all other things in the set are contingent it will be such that the necessary existence overrides all of the contingent existences. If the set is composed of only contingent existences, then it requires that which supplies existence. This can either be in the set of contingent existences or outside of the set. If it is inside the set, then this has already been elaborated upon. Or, [it could be] that it is a contingent existence such that it is the cause of the set, and the cause of the set is by extension the cause of all of its constituent parts. If it is inside the set [or is the set itself] – even though this is impossible – this line of argumentation could still be valid, so from one perspective then one will have fulfilled the object in making this conclusion (i.e. because this would have proven the existence of the necessary existence). This is because anything that is self-sufficient (i.e. the set in question) is a necessary existence. And the necessary existence cannot be this; it is also impossible that a contingent existence can exist outside the set, as the set is by definition a collation of all contingent existences. Therefore, it (the supplier of existence) must be outside of it as well as necessary in essence. Thus, the set of contingent existences has culminated in the need for a necessary existence outside of the set in order to explain it. It is not the case that every contingent effect has a contingent cause as a matter of infinite regress.[9]

The first stage of Ibn Sīnā's discourse is to establish 'existence' as the most foundational, transcendental, and universal category of analysis. The first major postulation which Ibn Sīnā makes is to state that 'it is not possible for there to be an infinite regress of causes for a contingent existence'.[10] Ibn Sīnā employs a set theory type of reasoning for this, gathering together all members of a specific description in one set and analysing that set thereafter. On this point regarding 'possible' or 'contingent' existences, Ibn Sīnā states:

> If they are all together and there is no necessary existence in the set, [we find that] upon exhaustive analysis [and whether or not it is finite or infinite], the set [of contingent things] can either be composed of contingent things or necessary things.[11]

Simply put, a set of one type of things excludes other types. For example, a set of chairs excludes tables. Likewise, a set of pens excludes pencils. Ultimately, this means that a set of contingent existences excludes necessary existences and vice versa. Ibn Sīnā states that if somehow a necessary existence can exist in the set of impossible existence (though

---

[9] Ibn Sīnā, A. (1937) *Al-Najāh*. Al-Maktabah al-Murtaḍawiyyah, p. 230.
[10] Ibid.
[11] Ibid.

this is logically impossible), this would be a counterintuitive proposition to make for anyone who aims to deny such a necessary existence. Ibn Sīnā goes on to suggest that just as it is as impossible for a necessary existence to be represented in a set of only contingent existences, it is also impossible for a contingent existence *not* to be represented by the set of all contingent existences. With this groundwork put in place, Ibn Sīnā concludes that 'the set of contingent existences has culminated in the need for a necessary existence outside of the set in order to explain it'.[12] Summarising the argument further, Herbert Davidson mentions Ibn Sīnā's argument as pointing that 'possibly existent beings are traceable to a necessary existence (by virtue of itself)...something exists which is a possible existence by virtue of itself; therefore something exists which is traceable to a necessary being by virtue of itself'.[13]

Notwithstanding this, it is perhaps a good place to start understanding the metaphysical compartmentalisations and how Ibn Sīnā categorises existence, as this effectively lays the groundwork for his argument. Regarding this matter, Ibn Sīnā starts the 6th chapter of *Metaphysics of the Cure* by defining what constitutes 'necessary existence' by stating:

> So we say that the necessary existence is uncaused, whereas a 'contingent existence' is caused, and that the necessary existence is necessary in all possible ways and perspectives conceivable. Its existence cannot be a result of the existence of anything else. If that were so, it would be as if each of those two things (i.e. the

---

[12] Ibid.
[13] Davidson, H. (1987). *Proofs for eternity, creation and the existence of God in medieval Islamic and Jewish philosophy*. Oxford University Press, p. 304.

9

supposed necessary existence in question and the thing which it results from) are equal in terms of existence and interdependent of each other. And it is not cogently possible for the necessary existence's existence to be as a result of many things. The necessary existence cannot cogently be 'the reality' that has any common aspect of it (with that which is not necessary). Thus, in order to be classified as 'necessary', the necessary existence cannot be added upon, constructed, mutable, divisible, or one of multiple contributors to its own existence which is specific to it.[14]

In *The Pointers and Reminders*, Ibn Sīnā starts off with a classification of that which is possible or 'contingent', *muḥāl* or 'impossible' (like a square circle), and necessary.[15] On a similar note, in his *Metaphysics* Ibn Sīnā moves on to speaking directly of the modal specialities of the necessary existence:

As for the necessary existence, it has no cause. This is because, if it had a cause, its existence would be because of it. Anything which is considered essentially by itself and its existence is not necessary in itself cannot be a 'necessary existence'…so it has been made clear that a necessary existence is uncaused. As a corollary to this, it is not possible that a thing is a necessary existence in and of itself and also because of another thing…Moreover, [regarding] anything that is a contingent existence in essence, both its existence or non-

[14] Ibn Sīnā, A. (1997) *Al-Shifā'*. Markaz al-Nashr, p. 50.
[15] Ibn Sīnā, A. (1957). *Al-Ishārāt wa al-tanbīhāt*. Cairo: Dar al-Maʿārif, p. 3.

existence would come about because of a cause. This is because if the [contingent] thing can be located, then its existence can be discerned from nothingness (or lack of its existence), and if it is not in existence, then its non-existence would be discernible from its existence. So, an exhaustive rendering of the options would suggest that its existence or lack of existence would either be caused because of something else or not. If it is from something else, then that something else is the cause of it. And if it is not from something else, then it is itself the necessary existence.[16]

In *The Pointers and Reminders*, Ibn Sīnā talks about a *jumlah* (roughly translated to a sequence or even a set) consisting of an infinite number of contingent things, arguing *ad absurdum* that such a set cannot be the necessary existence. Applying this to arguments posited by New Atheists, this part of the argument is one of the most potent and useful proofs in arguing against an infinite multiverse thesis. This thesis is often employed as a substitute for a necessary existence or 'God', a point that will be expanded on in following chapters. In the *Metaphysics,* Ibn Sīnā is most explicit in making a formal argument in *maqālah* (section) 8, chapters *1-3*. It merits consideration that Ibn Sīnā effectively ends his book with this argument, and in many ways earlier chapters seem to build up to this point. In this section, Ibn Sīnā argues *ad absurdum* for the impossibility of an infinite regress, doing so in two novel ways highlighted below: first, arguing for the impossibility of all 'middle causes' having the same modal status, and second, employing an argument from composition. As will be explained, these types of arguments are perhaps best placed to

---

[16] *Al-Shifā'*, pp. 50-51.

deal with atheistic interrogations which stipulate an infinite multiverse. After conceptualising a set of all existent things (the aforementioned *jumlah*), Ibn Sīnā posits that:

> [The] 'ultimate cause' cannot be the last in the set of causes, nor can it be in the middle. That is because the middle cause in the set can only cause one effect. In addition, the effect does not cause anything. And each thing of the three types at each extremity in the set [of existent things] has a specialised modal status. Thus, the specialised modal status of the thing at the end of the set is that it is not a cause for anything [by definition].[17]

To illustrate this argument, conceptualise a linear set from P to P10. Ibn Sīnā is simply stating that by logical necessity P5 can only be a cause for P6 in the set, and not for those things which come before it. P10 is not the cause for anything in this set. He continues this line of reasoning by stating:

> At the other extremity of the set (i.e. at the beginning of it) the cause (by definition) is the cause for all other things in that set. The specialised modal status of the thing which exists at the middle of the set is that it must be caused by one thing and be the cause for one thing.[18]

If the set is finite and linear, P5 must be caused by P4 and must be the cause of P6; this is the case even if the elements between P1-10 are multiple, for as Ibn Sīnā suggests:

> That is [the case] regardless of whether the thing(s) at the middle is one thing or more than

---

[17] Ibid, p. 243.
[18] Ibid.

one thing. If it is more than one thing(s), then it is either finite or infinite: if it is finite, then the set is between two extremities (i.e. the first cause and the final effect). Therefore, each of the things in between these two extremities will have a specialised status (which corresponds to the finitude of the set).[19]

Ibn Sīnā expands this argument of an infinite set in both *The Pointers* and *The Deliverance* by considering a circular finite set. Herbert Davidson addresses this point in his work on medieval *Kalām* (scholastic theology) entitled as *Proofs for Eternity*:

> ...a self-contained circular regress is shown to be absurd by an argument applying only to it. In the circular regress $x\ y\ z$, x would be a distant cause of z, and z would be the immediate cause of x. x would consequently be a distant cause of itself, which Avicenna regards as absurd. By the same token, x would be a distant effect of itself, which is equally absurd. And the point can be made again in a slightly different way, as follows: x would be dependent for its existence upon something-z-whose existence is posterior to it. But "when the existence of something depends upon the existence of something else that is essentially posterior to the first, the existence of the first is impossible." A self contained circular regress of causes cannot, therefore, exist.[20]

Having dealt with a finite set, Ibn Sīnā moves on to

---

[19] Ibid.
[20] *Proofs for eternity, creation and the existence of God in medieval Islamic and Jewish philosophy*, p. 302.

address the infinite regress objection, stating:

> If the set, on the other hand, is infinite, then such
> extremities (the first cause and final effect) will
> not have been realised, and all things in the set
> will have the [equivalent] status of the things
> between the two sets (i.e. they will not be first
> causes or final effects).[21]

On this rendering – and returning back to our P1-P10
example – P1, P5, and P10 are meaningless in an infinite set.
All Ps have the same modal specification, and they cannot
possibly be considered 'initiators', 'middle points', or 'final
effects'. Ibn Sīnā elaborates on this point by stating:

> [Regarding] this infinite set, if you add or
> subtract from it, its status as 'infinite' will
> remain the same. In this case [of the infinite set],
> it is not possible for the set of causes to exist
> without having a cause that is itself uncaused
> and originating. Accordingly, all of the things in
> the set will have the status of the middle things
> in the set (i.e. being neither final effect or first
> cause), and this is logically impossible.[22]

Ibn Sīnā, like Aristotle, was an eternalist. In other words,
he actually believed that the universe was pre-eternal. This
startling fact puts him at odds with many Islamic thinkers who
opposed such notions (most notably al-Ghazālī). Despite
believing in an eternal universe, Ibn Sīnā, like Aristotle, argued
quite clearly for the impossibility of an infinite regress of
causes.[23]

---

[21] *Al-Shifā'*, p. 243.
[22] Ibid, p. 264.
[23] *Proofs for eternity, creation and the existence of God in medieval Islamic and Jewish philosophy*, p. 301.

In addition to the argument from middle causes, Ibn Sīnā makes an argument from composition in the following manner:

> So we say [that] the necessary existence cannot be considered a 'composite construction' such that there is a certain 'whatness' attribute [attributed to it], and that such 'whatness' is itself the quality of necessity...it would be logically impossible that in such a 'whatness' there is an actual reality, for if it had a reality and that it was differentiated from the necessary existence then it would indicate that something unnecessary had brought about something necessary. And this would indicate that the thing in question is not, in fact, necessary.[24]

The argument from composition suggests that anything which is composed is generated and is therefore dependent. If there is a quality within something that makes it 'necessary' and capable of being extracted from while also being characterised with differentiation, then it would suggest that the entity in question is in need of it. As such, this would be enough proof to indicate the contingency of that entity. Taking Ibn Sīnā's premise that any composed entity that exists by its parts (and not by virtue of itself) is composite and therefore any composite is dependent,[25] the prospect of an infinite number of contingent things in existence becomes an impossible prospect to maintain. Hebert Davidson summarises this argument in the following way:

> Hence, on this alternative, "whether the group is finite or infinite," it stands in need of a factor that will continually "provide it with existence."

---

[24] *Al-Shifā'*, p. 366-7.
[25] *Proofs for eternity, creation and the existence of God in medieval Islamic and Jewish philosophy*, p. 287.

The factor, Avicenna assumes, must be either (β1) within the group or (β1) outside it. Assuming that the whole group is (β1) ultimately maintained by one of its own members would, however, be tantamount to assuming that the member in question is a cause of itself. For to be a cause of the existence of a group is "primarily" to be the cause of the individual members; and inasmuch as the supposed cause is itself one of the members, it would perforce be a cause of itself. Yet the supposed cause has already been assumed, as one of the members of the group, to be possibly existent; and the possibly existent is precisely what does not exist by reason of itself. Therefore, it could not be the cause of the collection of which it is one member.[26]

This point is particularly relevant to the discussion on the New Atheism movement and its interrogations of theism. In his three-part specialised podcast on Ibn Sīnā, Peter Adamson mentions the relevance of this argument to modern day discussions between theists and atheists. When discussing the part of Ibn Sīnā's argument in which he examines the implausibility of the entire set of existence being necessary if its parts are contingent, Adamson refers to Bertrand Russell's famous fallacy of composition objection. The latter will be revisited in greater detail in the chapter on objections. Adamson provides the example of a big clock made up of small parts and mentions that just because there are causes within the universe, it does not necessarily mean that the universe itself has a cause. Adamson explains that this:

...sounds like the sort of thing a modern-day

---

[26] Ibid, p. 301.

16

atheist may say. Avicenna is relaxed on this point. He sees that an opponent might raise this objection and, as if shrugging his shoulders, says that in that case, the opponent would just be giving him what he wants…after all, he is out to prove that there is a necessary existence. The opponent has actually admitted that – it's just that the opponent thinks that the necessary existence is the universe itself – the objection is no objection at all, but a capitulation.[27]

Having said this, Adamson explains that according to Ibn Sīnā, the universe (or the set of units) cannot be the necessary existence because:

> If a single necessary existent had parts, then something would need to distinguish those parts from one another. But then, by the same reasoning, we just used, the parts would wind up being different from one another, and then they would not be necessary – but how can a necessary existent have contingent parts?[28]

When using Ibn Sīnā's arguments pastorally, it is important to note the threshold at which an interlocutor has shifted away from atheistic explanations and moved towards explanations which are somewhat more commensurate with deism or classical theism. The purpose of these logical arguments is not to convince the interlocutor of all of the attributes of God in accordance with scripture by arguing (as Ibn Sīnā does above) from first principles. Rather, the prime objective is to demonstrate to an atheistic detractor that a

---

[27] Adamson, P. (2013). *By all means necessary. Avicenna on God. History of philosophy without any gaps.* 6:37. Available at: https://historyofphilosophy.net/avicenna-life-works.
[28] Ibid, 10:38.

worldview which does not acknowledge the status of an originator of existence is deficient and can be easily repudiated.

To summarise, Ibn Sīnā's *Burhān* argument can be categorised as a cause-based argument from contingency. The thrust of the argument is that existence cannot contain only contingent actualities, as contingent existence cannot bring rise to itself. A collection of contingent existences – whether finite or infinite – is not self-sufficient or necessary, as such a collection is made up of many component parts. If there is anything to differentiate Part A from Part B, such a thing would indicate the non-necessity of Part A or Part B, as well as the 'whole' which is being described. For this reason, the necessary existent cannot be composed of component parts. In addition, because of this reason, a set of contingent existences – whether finite or infinite – cannot be a necessary existence. Therefore, there is the requirement for a necessary existence to subsist outside of the set of contingent existence, which ultimately causes this set, as well as all of its members. Such a necessary existence which is outside the set of contingent existences must be self-sufficient; it requires nothing to generate or cause it, as the failure to be such would necessarily indicate its contingency.

In application

Richard, who I have described in the introduction, may reject the proposition of a necessary existence in exchange for an infinite multiverse. The question that may be posed to Richard is whether such a multi-verse is self-sufficient or dependent. If Richard replies that it is dependent, then the question is: is it dependent on something which is dependent or something which is independent (self-sufficient). If independent, then there is agreement at least on the point that there exists an 'independent entity'. If dependent, then is there an infinite regress of dependent things? If so, what does such infinite regress depend on? Richard may say that it depends upon nothing. If this is so, Richard is admitting the infinite multiverse is independent, again a point of agreement as Richard would be agreeing to the existence of something self-sufficient. The major point of disagreement relates to what the independent being is. One can argue that anything composed of detachable/attachable parts is dependent, and since the universe is composed in this way, therefore the universe is dependent. The same thing can be said about an infinite multiverse. This will be fleshed out in the chapters to come.

Chapter 2
MEDIEVAL RECEPTION

In this chapter, I will assess the responses of some Muslim and Christian theologians to Ibn Sīnā's arguments. Among the Muslim theologians, I will refer to the writings of al Ghazālī, Ibn Rushd, and Ibn Taymiyyah, all of whom had intriguing responses to Ibn Sīnā. Many of these scholarly responses to Ibn Sīnā's arguments can be accessed in English, with the exception of Ibn Taymiyyah. The latter's *Kalām*-based arguments for God's existence are widely untranslated or disregarded within academia. His contribution is particularly valuable, as he deals not only with the theoretical elements of the argument, but also their pastoral and apologetic applications. Moreover, although the Mu'tazilites engaged actively with the theological area of proving God's existence, it appears that the major argument they employed was *dalīl al-a'rāḍ wa ḥudūth al-ajsām,* which translates to 'the proof from accidents and commencement of bodies'.[29] This specific argument goes beyond the remit of this book, and requires a separate treatment altogether. Finally, I will then assess some of the uses of Ibn Sīnā's *Burhān* in the Christian tradition, with particular reference to Thomas Aquinas and John Duns Scotus.

The most important points of extrapolation from all of these thinkers are reformulations or criticisms of the argument. These can be considered as a means to strengthen the

---

[29] Jabbār, A. (1987). *Kitāb al-majmū' fī muḥīt bi al-taklīf.* Beirut: Dār al-Mashriq.

argument, refine it, or even add to it. Despite the objections that many of these thinkers raise with certain formulations of Ibn Sīnā's argument, practically all of them converge on his conclusion of the reality of a 'necessary existence', which explains all other forms of existence. Finally, this section argues that the conclusion of a 'necessary existence' is so pervasive within interreligious intellectual circles that it may very well be the most agreed upon belief between all monotheists in the history of theological philosophy.

Restating Ibn Sīnā's Argument in a Nutshell

Ibn Sīnā's *Burhān* argument goes as follows. There is existence. Existence is of three types: possible (contingent), necessary, and impossible. Impossible existences (like squared circles) cannot exist. There cannot be only contingent existences in existence, as they would require something else in order to cause them into existence. There cannot be a finite or infinite series of contingent existences, as such a series would be composed of many differentiated and dependent members. The differentiation and dependent aspects found in the different members of the series indicate that the finite or infinite series itself cannot be necessary. Instead, it must be contingent. Thus, only a necessary existence can cause or ultimately explain why any contingent existences happen to occur.

Al-Ghazālī's Rejection of an Infinite Regress of things and his insistence on a Godly Will

Al-Ghazālī was perhaps the most famous critic of Ibn Sīnā in the Muslim world, with his publication of *Tahāfut al-Falāsifah* (*The Incoherence of the Philosophers*), where he directly attacked Ibn Sīnā's beliefs. Al-Ghazālī's criticism was so scathing that it led him to excommunicate Ibn Sīnā for four different reasons outlined at the end of his book, the most

21

relevant of which surrounds Ibn Sīnā's views on the eternity of the universe. In what will follow I will outline the critical differences found between the approaches of Ibn Sīnā and al-Ghazālī in demonstrating God's existence. Particular focus will be given to the subjects of infinite regress and eternality, as well as arguments against emanationism and Godly will. Though al-Ghazālī does not directly challenge any of the premises of Ibn Sīnā's overall argument mentioned above, nevertheless his criticisms of Ibn Sīnā's general approach are just as important. After all, they give the theistic apologist more argumentative options than would be afforded by just relying on Ibn Sīnā's articulations of the *Burhān* alone.

As it relates to the infinite regress, al-Ghazālī makes the argument that 'anything susceptible to greater or lesser is finite'. This is concurrent with the proofs already employed by the likes of John of Philoponus.[30] Ibn Sīnā was an eternalist (believing the universe is pre-eternal), as well as an emanationist (believing that the universe emanates from God necessarily). Expressed in another manner, Ibn Sīnā believed that God's bringing of the universe into existence is analogous to the Sun emitting light. In this simile, the light represents the universe and the Sun symbolises God.[31] Al-Ghazālī, however, considers eternalism to be inconsistent with an omnipotent God, as it renders him impotent to prevent things from coming into existence, or from not coming into existence in the first place.[32] Indeed, al-Ghazālī (alongside other Ash'arites who preceded him) made arguments from 'particularisation' which aim to establish the divine will through cosmological proofs.

---

[30] *Proofs for eternity, creation and the existence of God in medieval Islamic and Jewish philosophy*, p. 118.
[31] Leaman, O. (2000). *A brief introduction to Islamic philosophy*. Polity Press, p. 41.
[32] *Proofs for eternity, creation and the existence of God in medieval Islamic and Jewish philosophy*, p. 4; Griffel, F. (2009). *Al-Ghazali's philosophical theology*. Oxford University Press, p.185.

Within this context, they give examples like those of rotating planets in space that had the potential of rotating the other way.[33] Exploring the Ash'arite argument from particularisation is important, as it is almost totally absent in discourses in the philosophy of religion (as an argument for the will of God), despite the high-level scope the argument holds. Unfortunately, it could be said that the Ash'arites were not well-suited to deal with possible determinist objections (to be dealt with in the chapter on objections). This is because many of its key thinkers, including al Ghazālī, were occasionalist in inclination, thereby anticipating David Hume by arguing that the connection between cause and effect is not necessary. Oftentimes, they use the example of fire that seemingly causes combustion to cotton, while in reality arguing that causation is from God directly.[34]

Occasionalism, of course, weakens the first premise of al-Ghazālī's own argument, which states that: 'Everything that begins to exist has a cause, the universe began to exist, therefore the universe has a cause'.[35] This is because the premise 'everything that begins to exist has a cause' cannot be established inductively if al-Ghazālī actually argues – in other works – that causes are directly from God. If these causes are actually what are being referred to, then al-Ghazālī may be accused of begging the question. In refutation of this viewpoint, the Ḥanbalite scholar Ibn Taymiyyah argues that secondary causation does not endanger the independence of God, namely by establishing the difference between 'direct causation and indirect causation'.[36] Ibn Taymiyyah reasons that

---

[33] Al-Ghazālī, A. (2003). *Tahāfut al-falāsifah*. Kotaib, p. 97; Proofs *for eternity, creation and the existence of God in medieval Islamic and Jewish philosophy*, p. 118.

[34] *Al-Ghazali's philosophical theology,* p. 172; Sorabji, R. (1984). *Time, creation and the continuum*. Bloomsbury, p. 299.

[35] Al-Ghazālī, A. (2008). *Al-Iqtiṣād fī al-'itiqād*. Cairo: Dar Al-Basāir, pp. 201-202.

things in the world are contingent in and of themselves and only necessary because of their connection to the necessary existence.[37] This is to say that things in the universe are contingent in abstraction, and determined in their connection with the necessary existence. Although New Atheists (and other non-theists) have not made this formal objection to the contingency argument in the literature, it can be anticipated that the determinists among them would take such a course of action. A key example in this regard may be Sam Harris, who makes the case for determinism in his book *Free Will*. On this line of reasoning the status of an object as 'contingent' will be put into question on account of it being determined by antecedent causes, where it could not be in any other way. By differentiating things that could not be any other way in abstraction (in and of themselves) from those things that could not be any other way because of another thing (say an uninterrupted causal chain or an uncaused determiner), one can circle this objection.

Another subject of enquiry is al-Ghazālī's suspicion of Ibn Sīnā's modal categories as being relevant to the real world. Regarding this, Griffel states that 'Al-Ghazali questions the assumption of an ontological coherence between this world and our knowledge of it. Certain predications – which, for Avicenna, apply to things in the real world – apply, for Al-Ghazali, only to human judgements'.[38] This 'suspicion' is concurrent with the Kantian objection to the ontological argument. It cannot be reasoned, however, that al-Ghazālī did not believe in possibility and necessity as existing in the 'real world'. For he and the Ash'arites that preceded him made an argument from particularisation, as explained by Griffel:

---

[36] Ibn Taymiyyah, A. (1986). *Minhāj al-sunnah al-nabawiyyah*. M. R. Salim (Ed.). Maktabah Ibn Taymiyyah, p. 146.
[37] Ibid, pp. 146-147.
[38] *Al-Ghazali's philosophical theology*, p. 164.

The idea of particularisation (*takhsis*) implicitly includes an understanding of possible worlds that are different from ours. The process of particularisation actualises a given one of many alternatives. Yet the alternatives to this world – Which would be: "X comes into existence at a time different from when X comes into existence" are not explicitly expressed or imagined. The Kalam concept of preponderance (*tarjih*), however, explicitly discusses the assumption of a possible worlds....[39]

Griffel goes on to postulate that al-Ghazālī's version of this particularisation has 'strong overtones of Avicenna's ontology: because everything in the world can be perceived as nonexisting, its nonexistence is itself equally possible as its existence. Existent things necessarily need something that "tip the scales" its existence...God is this preponderator (*murajjih*) who in this sense determines the existence of anything in the world'.[40] The argument of particularisation is of great significance, as it allows theists to make an argument for a volitional God. Such a feature is not available through a *Burhān* argument alone and is therefore invaluable to any theistic apologist.

Ibn Rushd (Averroes), the Modal Categories, and the True Nature of Possibility

Ibn Rushd's critique of Ibn Sīnā's argument presented above does not relate much to the flow of the argument. Instead, it largely lies in the way Ibn Sīnā defines the modal categories, especially the category of *mumkin al-wujūd* (possible or contingent existences). In his famous invocation of Aristotle,

---

[39] Ibid, p. 170.
[40] Ibid.

Ibn Rushd mentions that 'it is impossible for any science to demonstrate the existence of its own subject matter'.[41] In his *Pointers*, Ibn Sīnā defines possible (contingent) existence as something which is 'not impossible and not necessary'.[42] In addition, he indicates that if such a contingent existence is not in existence no logical absurdities would occur. Ibn Rushd claims that in order for Ibn Sīnā's *Burhān* argument to be properly made, an appropriate definition of possible existence or *mumkin al-wujūd* must be adopted, namely 'what is generated or destroyed'. This must be the analytical starting point, for it is empirically attested.[43] If one does not start with this kind of definition, one will be at risk of equivocating between that which is contingent and that which is caused. In fact, Ibn Rushd accuses Ibn Sīnā of equivocating between causes and contingencies; within this critical discussion he states that contingent things are broader than causes.[44] Importantly, Ibn Rushd accuses Ibn Sīnā of claiming that contingent things are caused and that in his view this distinction 'is not a division that considers the qua existent'.[45]

Bearing Ibn Rushd's criticism in mind, in my own presentation of arguments I will make sure that I differentiate between causes, dependent things, and contingent things.

Thomas Aquinas and the Third Way

Ibn Sīnā's *Burhān* was influential to the degree that it appears in the works of Thomas Aquinas.[46] In addition to Ibn Rushd,

---

[41] *Proofs for eternity, creation and the existence of God in medieval Islamic and Jewish philosophy*, p. 312.

[42] Ibn Sīnā, A. (1957). *Al-Ishārāt wa al-tanbīhāt*. Cairo: Dar al-Ma'ārif, p. 19.

[43] *Proofs for eternity, creation and the existence of God in medieval Islamic and Jewish philosophy*, p. 333.

[44] Ibid, 332.

[45] Ibid.

the approach of Aquinas is commensurate with that of his Ḥanbalite contemporary Ibn Taymiyyah, who, in his *Sharḥ al 'Aqīdah al-Aṣfahāniyyah* (Explanation of the Creed of Aṣfahān) prefers a form of cosmological reasoning to demonstrate God's existence.[47] When presenting his viewpoint, Aquinas states:

> The third way is based on what need not be and on what must be, and runs as follows. Some of the things we come across can be but need not be, for we find them being generated and destroyed, thus sometimes in being and sometimes not. Now everything cannot be like this, for a thing that need not be was once not; and if everything need not be, once upon a time there was nothing. But if that were true there would be nothing even now, because something that does not exist can only begin to exist through something that already exists. If nothing was in being nothing could begin to be, and nothing would be in being now, which is clearly false. Not everything then is the sort of thing that need not be; some things must be and these may or may not owe this necessity to something else. But just as we proved that a series of agent [efficient] causes can't go on forever, so also a series of things which must be and owe this to other things. So we are forced to postulate something which of itself must be, owing this to nothing outside itself, but being itself the cause that other things must be. And this is what

[46] Owens, J. (1974). Aquinas and the five ways. *The Monist*, 58(1), Oxford University Press, p. 20.

[47] Ibn Taymiyyah, A. (2009) *Sharḥ al-'aqīdah al-aṣfahāniyyah*. Riyadh: Maktabah Dār al Minhāj, pp. 55-65.

everyone calls God.[48]

Aquinas's argument, which can also be seen as an argument from contingency, can be summarised as follows: Contingent things are things which could be or not be. We see things around us which are contingent. If something can be or not be, it is not deemed necessary, but instead is caused by something else. There cannot be a world of only contingent things, as the explanation of such things lies with something other than itself. We cannot have an infinite series of contingent things, just as we cannot have an infinite series of causes. For this reason, we must have something self-sufficient and necessary which must 'be of itself' and owe such being to nothing 'outside of itself'. Like Ibn Rushd, Aquinas defines *imkān* or possibility strictly using generation and destructibility. Unlike Ibn Sīnā, however, Aquinas does not employ the form of *Tarkīb* argument which argues that anything with distinguishable and dependent parts cannot be necessary. It may be argued that the lack of this feature makes the argument more susceptible to the fallacy of composition.

A possible way around this is the use of the concepts of potentiality and actuality. According to Aquinas, 'potentiality is actualized only by something already in actuality'.[49] It can be argued using this concept that since the universe is constantly changing, this is evidence of its potentiality. Anything potential must require an external cause or actualiser. This argument has been used to great effect by Christian apologists such as Edward Feser, who argues at length that God is the necessary actualiser.[50] Notably, Feser employed this argument against Graham Oppy to good effect in an online discussion entitled

[48] Davies, B. (2001). Aquinas's third way. *New Blackfriars.* 82(968), p. 450.
[49] Owens, J. (1974). Aquinas and the five ways. *The Monist, 58*(1), Oxford University Press, p. 21.
[50] Feser, E. (2017). *Five proofs of the existence of God.* San Francisco: Ignatius Press, p. 115.

Are There Any Good Arguments for God? During this discussion, Oppy could not devise a solution to the problem of potentialities becoming actualities.

One of the biggest advantages of Aquinas's third way and those who have commented on it is that it allows us to gauge an entire stream of Western philosophical criticism. This is practically expedient, as it chiefly relates to anticipated objections and reactions to these kinds of arguments in dialectic discourse. On this point, Michael Augros summarises the three main objections to the third way by stating:

> (1) the premise that "What is possible not to be at some time is not" appears to be unknowable, (2) when Aquinas says "if therefore all things (omnia) are possible not to be, at some time nothing was in things" he is guilty of the quantifier shift, and (3) granting the entire argument, Aquinas has no right to conclude the existence of anything other than matter, which one might well believe is a self-necessary being'.[51]

As seen in the previous chapter (and putting aside the validity or lack thereof of these interrogations), Ibn Sīnā does not present the argument in a way that makes it susceptible to these criticisms. For example, the proposition 'what is possible not to be at some time is not' does not feature at all in Ibn Sīnā's version of the argument. The idea that 'If therefore all things are possible not to be, at some time nothing was in things' would not seem to be commensurate with Ibn Sīnā's reasoning at all.

As for the third point of criticism associated with

---

[51] Augros, M. (2006). Aquinas's "tertia via". *Pontificia Studiorum Universitas a Sancto Thomas Aquinate. 83*(4), p. 769.

materiality, Anthony Kenny states that 'in order to show that the uncaused everlasting being must be God, he offers no proof, and we may ask why might it not be perpetual, indestructible matter?'.[52] Al-Ghazālī, however, anticipates this line of reasoning in his *Tahāfut* by asking:

> But as for [you philosophers], what is there to prevent you from [upholding] the doctrine of the materialists – namely, that the world is eternal, that it likewise has no cause and no maker, that only temporal events have a cause, that nobody in the world is originated and nobody annihilated, but [that] which occurs temporally is but forms and accidents?[53]

Ibn Sīnā deals with the contention of materiality in considerable detail, as shown through the composition argument. As mentioned hitherto, Ibn Sīnā has a separate argument of composition responding to this in order to show that the uncaused and everlasting being must be God. This acts as a necessary corollary to his argument for an uncaused causer. Furthermore, this would indicate the impossibility of something which has a material form as being a necessary existence. It would seem therefore that the three major objections found in Western philosophy against Aquinas's Third Way – as mentioned by Augros above – are nonfactors when returning to Ibn Sīnā's original arguments.

---

[52] Kenny, A. (2014) *The five ways: St. Thomas Aquinas's proofs of God's existence.* Routledge, p. 69.
[53] Al-Ghazālī . (2000). *The Incoherence of the Philosophers*, trans., Michael Marmura . Provo, Utah: Brigham Young University Press, p. 123.

Ibn Taymiyyah's Part/Attribute Quandary and Apologetic Recommendations

Ibn Taymiyyah – who prefers the argument to be made cosmologically – makes a clear distinction between a 'part' and an 'attribute'. According to Ibn Taymiyyah, a part is something that is materially added or removed from a substratum, like planks of wood that a whole [ship] depends upon for its existence.[54] Anything that is constituted by material parts like these must be composed or generated. Considering that the universe – or a multiverse – would fit this description, it would follow that a universe or multiverse would be composed or generated. Ibn Taymiyyah goes on to argue that the attributes of God are *talāzumī* (necessary) such that they cannot be imagined in another way.[55] Although Ibn Taymiyyah himself does not endorse it in ontological terms, nevertheless he renders the composition argument possible in terms similar to Ibn Sīnā's set theory type formulations explored in the previous chapter.

These medieval discussions have already been a staple part of the atheist versus theist discourse, especially with the rise of agnosticism in recent years. Ironically, it was Anthony Kenny himself – who was acting in his capacity as a moderator – challenged Richard Dawkins with this line of thinking. This was during the latter's debate with Rowan Williams – the Archbishop of Canterbury at that time – regarding Dawkins' argument of a complex God, where the example of an electric razor and a cutthroat razor was invoked. On this point, Kenny stated that 'the cutthroat razor is simpler in design but has more complex powers than the electric razor', after which Dawkins had no response but to plead ignorance, thereby demonstrating

---

[54] Ibn Taymiyyah, A. (2009) *Sharḥ al-ʿaqīdah al-aṣfahāniyyah*. Riyadh: Maktabah Dār al Minhāj, p. 37.
[55] Ibid, pp. 37-38.

31

the effectiveness of this line of reasoning.[56] One can see how making mereological distinctions – like those hitherto explored – is an essential part of making the argument from composition. If one defines a 'part' in a way that includes 'attributes', the apologetic mission may halt at a point of deism, as the affirmation of Godly attributes that are known through revelation becomes both redundant and superfluous.

Many arguments for God's existence can be quite complicated for an audience consisting of laypeople. They can be off-putting in pastoral settings, where the common folk just want to resolve atheistic doubts. In the Islamic golden age, the traditionalist Ibn Taymiyyah was most disapproving of employing overly complicated arguments when addressing lay people. He argued that they should be limited to an audience with an analytic background, interestingly pointing out that for 'some people, every time the proof is more explicated and detailed, with more logical premises, it was more useful to them…and with this kind of person, one should use a detailed *Kalām* approach or other such analytic approach which they would be used to'.[57] In another work entitled as *Mas'alah Ḥudūth al-ʿĀlam* (The Issue of the Beginning of the World), he states that the best way to convince a layperson of God is to use the most basic reasoning possible. Commenting on one of the Qur'an's many rhetorical questions, 'Or were they created from nothing or are they their own creators?' (Qur'an, 52:35), Ibn Taymiyyah states:

> This categorisation is the easiest and clearest way that one can reason the existence of a creator with the most minimal amount of

---

[56] The Archbishop of Canterbury. (2012). *Dialogue with Richard Dawkins, Rowan Williams and Anthony Kenny* [video]. 01:56:40. Available at: https://www.youtube.com/watch?v=bow4nnh1Wv0.
[57] Ibn Taymiyyah, A. (2005) Al-Radd ʿAla Al-Mantiqiyyīn. Beirut: Muassasat Al-Rayyā, pp. 373-374.

introspection. This is because the slave knows that he once did not exist, and that he came into existence after he did not exist…He also knows that he did not create himself or bring himself into existence, and this is known as a matter of critical certainty… He also knows that his creation could not be without a creator, and that there is no cause without effect… If he knows this, then he will know how to reason the existence of the heavens and the Earth.[58]

Al-Ghazālī makes a similar observation in his exegesis of the same verse referenced by Ibn Taymiyyah.[59] Introducing the doubter to simple questions such as 'do you think it is possible that the universe could come from nothing?' or 'is the universe dependent or independent?' are useful analytical starting points. Arguing for the impossibility of causal or dependent things may be enough to arrive at the conclusion that an independent entity responsible for all other things in existence is necessary to explain anything.

Duns Scotus's Contribution to the Argument

Duns Scotus begins his argument in a similar manner to al-Ghazālī and Ibn Tamiyyah. However, he then explicates two types of arguments (with one being cosmological, and the other being ontological) in order to produce an inescapable conclusion. Rega Wood summarises Scotus' argument in the following way:

(1) Something can be produced.

(2) Everything that is produced is produced

[58] Ibn Taymiyyah, A. (2012) *Mas'alah ḥudūth al-ʿālam*. Dār al-Bashāʾir al-Islāmiyyah, pp. 49-50.
[59] Al-Ghazālī, A. (2003). *Al-Iqtiṣād fī al-ʿitiqād*. Kotaib, p.39.

either by itself, nothing, or some other cause.

(3) Nothing can be produced from nothing.

(4) Nothing can produce itself.

(5) Therefore, something is produced by another cause, which we will call a.

(6) Either a is an uncaused cause or it is not.

(7) If a is an uncaused cause, this suffices as proof.

(8) If a is not an uncaused cause, then given steps (2-4), it must be produced by another cause, which we call b.

(9) But it is impossible to have an infinite series of causes preceding each other.

(10) Therefore, the procession must halt at some uncaused cause.[60]

Crucially, Scotus differentiates between accidentally ordered causes and essentially ordered causes. In the case of accidentally ordered causes, if one stops the other will not cease to exist. In the case of essentially ordered causes this is not the case. For example, a father may have a son, and the son may have another son. The grandfather may die, while both the son and the grandson will continue to exist. In this way, the son of the father and his own son can continue to exist despite the antecedent cause ceasing to exist.[61] Like Aristotle and Ibn Sīnā, Scotus argues strongly against the possibility of an infinite regress of essentially ordered causes.[62] Scotus's argument has

---

[60] Wood, R. (1987). Scotus's Argument for the Existence of God. *Franciscan Institute Publications, 47*, pp. 258- 259.
[61] Ibid, p. 260.
[62] Ibid; Ross, J. (2002). Duns Scotus on natural theology. In Thomas Williams (Ed.), *The Cambridge Companion to Duns Scotus*. Cambridge University Press, p. 198.

also been presented in the following manner:

(1) If an independent entity (call it *a*) can fail to exist, then something incompatible with it (call it *b*) can exist, for one of two contradictories is always true.

(2) Something incompatible with an independent entity cannot exist because everything that exists is either independent or dependent (i.e. from itself or from another).

(3) But *b* cannot be independent, since [if *b* is possible and independent], then it actually exists independently – from the third conclusion (conclusion 4 in *De primo principio*).

(4) And if *b* is independent, then its possibility implies its actual existence, and its possibility would imply that two logically incompatible beings would actually exist.

(5) *b* cannot be dependent.

(6) For nothing incompatible with something that exists can receive being from a cause, unless it receives from its cause a more potent being than that which it is incompatible with – [in this case *a*],

(7) But *a* is uncaused, and hence it is more potent than any being with a cause, since something caused owes its being to another entity.

(8) [Therefore, *b* cannot come into existence as a dependent being, since it could not receive more potent being than *a* from any cause]. (9) Therefore, *b* cannot exist, and *a* cannot fail to

exist.[63]

To transform this into a pure argument from necessity, one needs to only transform references from 'caused things' into 'dependent things'. Expressed in one line, the argument against infinite regress is simply that 'there cannot be an infinite regress of dependent things'. One may also effectively make a causation argument upon a parallel track – a suggestion made by Ibn Ṭufayl.[64] Doing so will have the net effect of rendering the argumentative target smaller and more difficult to attack for interlocutors in polemical or apologetic settings. As it will be covered in much more detail later, the objections relating to causation would simply be irrelevant to at least one form of the argument.

In this chapter, we have seen many of the sophisticated methods of demonstration employed by theologians and philosophers. In particular we have analysed the arguments of al-Ghazālī, Ibn Rushd (Averroes), Ibn Taymiyyah, Aquinas, and Duns Scotus. This is by no means an exhaustive list of important contributors or detractors to the argument put forward by Ibn Sīnā. Other theologians, such as al-Ṭūsī, Fakhr al-Dīn al-Rāzī, al-Masʿūdī, as well as many in the Muʿtazalite tradition have written commentaries on the *The Pointers* or have addressed Ibn Sīnā's *Burhān* argument in length. Many of these works are already available in the English language. Conspicuously absent from this chapter is also Maimonides, through whom Aquinas was introduced to Ibn Sīnā's argument. We have also been able to establish that objections expressed against Aquinas's contingency argument are not applicable to Ibn Sīnā's particular version. Moreover, the importance of defining the modal categories has been made clear to us by

---

[63] Ibid, p. 273.
[64] *Proofs for eternity, creation and the existence of God in medieval Islamic and Jewish philosophy*, p. 4.

almost all of the thinkers we have analysed. That being said, the fact that genii from varied religious traditions agree with at least one rendition of this argument speaks to the immense explanatory scope that such an argument has.

In application

Betty may not be convinced that the universe is contingent. Using Aquinas's lines of argumentation, one may be able to suggest to Betty that the universe is contingent because it is in constant change. Anything in constant change is potential and cannot be purely actual. Anything which is potential requires an outside cause. Some of the trauma Betty had suffered had been at the hands of her own family members. It may be that Betty may feel intimidated or distrustful of religious authority figures. It may also be that religion represents a greater authority that Betty disdains. Of course, it may be that Betty is genuinely not convinced with the arguments or that she doesn't want to be convinced by any argument that leads to religious living. It is impossible to assess Betty's intentions and psychoanalytic state. When interacting with Betty, I have found that the best way to be is as authentic as possible. To create a positive relationship with Betty.

Chapter 3

MODERN USAGES OF COSMOLOGICAL AND ONTOLOGICAL ARGUMENTS

In this chapter, I will critically examine some of the pre-existing literature available on the contingency argument made 'ontologically' in the field of Philosophy of Religion. I will assess whether it is fit for use in apologetic, polemic, and pastoral purposes. In addition, I will further evaluate some articulations of the cosmological argument and their relevance to the *Burhān,* which can itself be presented as a cosmological argument. Looking through certain arguments, I will critically assess which of the arguments is most easily stated and timeless, while also having the most explanatory scope and being least susceptible to refutation. These four conditions are of vital importance to the arguments, especially in regard to their use in pastoral and apologetic settings.

In the subsequent chapter, I will present my own rendition of these arguments, while using the *Burhān* as my guide. Although some of the arguments mentioned in this chapter can still be effective in such settings, I intend to demonstrate how the vulnerabilities of these arguments make the *Burhān* a better choice considering the conditions mentioned above.

Cosmological Arguments

Cosmological arguments – most notably the *Kalām* argument

presented by William Lane Craig – have been at the centre of much of the contemporary discourse around the validity of theism. As discussed in the previous chapter, Craig reiterates al-Ghazālī's argument that 'whatever begins to exist has a cause; the universe began to exist, and therefore the universe has a cause'.[65] The fact that the argument has generated much controversy – both within academia and public debate circles – indicates both its popularity and effectiveness. In order for the second premise of the argument to be sustained, Craig has made a series of arguments defending causality, which includes a static theory of time, the impossibility of an actual infinite, as well as posited arguments against quantum notions of a 'loosened' (or non-existent) causality.[66] For example, in his book *Time and Eternity*, Craig makes the following argument relating to the special theory of relativity:

1. Either the Einsteinian relativity interpretation or the Minkowskian space-time interpretation of STR is correct.

2. If the Minkowskian space-time interpretation of STR is correct, then

3. a static theory of time is correct and the Einsteinian relativity interpretation of STR is not correct.

4. Therefore, a static theory of time is correct.[67]

Employing these kinds of arguments may be an unnecessary encumbrance for advocates of theism. This is because the argument depends on disproving actual infinities in the real world in order to prove the universe has a beginning. To accomplish this, Craig has to argue against a legitimate

[65] Al-Ghazālī, A. (2008). *Al-Iqtiṣād fī al-ʿitiqād*, pp. 201-202; Craig, W. (1979). *Kalam cosmological argument*. Macmillan.
[66] Reichenbach, B. (2004). *Cosmological Argument*. [online]: https://plato.stanford.edu/entries/cosmological-argument/.
[67] Craig, W. (2001). *Time and eternity*. Crossway Books, p. 173.

mathematical interpretation of infinite sets (namely Cantorian interpretations) or alternatively show how they are not applicable in the real world.[68] If one is making the argument and is not well-acquainted with mathematics or the philosophy underpinning mathematics, the atheist interlocutor (who may be more educated on these subjects) may cite opposing interpretations and ultimately derail his opponent's argument.

The same thing may be said of relying on scientific proofs in order to prove the second premise of the *Kalām* argument, or the general idea that the universe has a beginning. For example, in *New Proofs for the Existence of God,* Robert J. Spitzer dedicates a considerable portion of his book to proving the occurrence of the Big Bang, the second law of thermodynamics, 'why a bouncing universe cannot have been bouncing forever', and similar topics.[69] The corrigible nature of science and volatile changes that occur in our understanding of physics not only require apologists to have a strong grasp of these fields, but may even lead to the understanding that the evidence presented today will be contradicted by future discoveries. In this way, such arguments do not fulfil the timeless criterion which is necessary for the continued relevance of theistic arguments. As we will see in our section in which the argument is presented, it may be unnecessary to engage with the interlocutor on the point of infinity. The same can be said for the case of the *Kalām* argument if one simply makes an argument from composition, a matter which has already been discussed.

---

[68] *Cosmological Argument.* [online]:
https://plato.stanford.edu/entries/cosmological-argument/.
[69] Spitzer, R. (2010). *New proofs for existence of God.* Wm. B. Eermans Publishing Co, pp. 22-27.

Leibniz and the Principle of Sufficient Reason

Many of the issues that one may have with the *Kalām* cosmological argument are overcome with Leibniz's contingency argument, an argument that can be made both cosmologically and ontologically. Leibniz's argument is not only consistent with the *Burhān* but contributes to it by introducing a general 'explanatory principle' referred to as the principle of sufficient reason, abbreviated as PSR.[70] Pruss summarises the argument in the following steps: '(1) Every contingent fact has an explanation. (2) There is a contingent fact that includes all other facts. (3) Therefore, there is an explanation of this fact'.[71] Pruss goes on to argue that the PSR is 'self-evident',[72] comparing it to the law of the excluded middle in axiomatic logic. As with the *Burhān*, the argument terminates with something that explains everything else in existence without requiring an explanation itself.

The simplicity of this argument makes it fit for use in apologetic and pastoral settings. However, the term 'explanation' may seem inappropriate, especially in cosmological examples. Moreover, the use of the term 'possible worlds' (as given in the system of S5 Modal logic) confers vulnerability upon the argument, as it opens the doors to 'modal nihilism,' the like of which was famously elaborated upon by W. V. Quine in his work *The Web of Belief.* Modal nihilism (and other such forms of modal scepticisms) can and have been refuted with considerable ease. A rejection of the modal categories (or indeed logic, mathematics, or any *a priori* truth) disarms Quine of the ability to use such tools in order to repudiate them.[73] Nevertheless, in order to sidestep this

---

[70] Pruss, W. (2009). The Leibnizian cosmological argument in *The Blackwell Companion to Natural Theology*. Blackwell, p. 25.
[71] Ibid.
[72] Ibid, p. 26.
[73] O'Connor, T. (2012). *Theism and Ultimate Explanation.* Oxford:

objection, I intend to produce at least one version of the argument without making reference to either causality or modality.

Ontological Arguments: Alvin Plantinga's 'Victorious Argument'

Ontological arguments for the existence of God could be said to have had a relatively less impact on public discourse. Alvin Plantinga, who himself employs a 'victorious' modal ontological argument, states:

> Our verdict on these reformulated versions of St. Anselm's argument must be as follows. They cannot, perhaps, be said to *prove* or *establish* their conclusion. But since it is rational to accept their central premise, they do show that it is rational to accept that conclusion.[74]

Using modal logic, Plantinga attempts to reformulate the ontological argument of a 'maximally perfect being', which was first famously elaborated by Anselm of Canterbury. Anselm's argument runs as follows:

(1) God exists in the realm of understanding but not in reality.

(2) Existence in reality is greater than existence in the mind alone.

(3) God's existence in reality is conceivable.

(4) If God did exist in reality, then he would be greater than he is in (1) and (2).

(5) It is conceivable that there be a being greater

Blackwell Publishing, p. 11.
[74] Plantinga, A. (1974). *The nature of necessity.* Clarendon Press, p. 221.

than God is in (3) and (4).

(6) It is conceivable that there is a being greater than the being about which nothing greater can be conceived (5), by the definition of 'God'.

(7) It is false that it is conceivable that there is a being greater than the being about which nothing greater can be conceived.

Since (6) and (7) contradict each other, we may conclude that (8) It is false that God exists in the understanding but not in reality.

So, if God exists in the understanding, he also exists in reality; but clearly enough he does exist in the understanding, as even the fool will testify; therefore, he exists in reality as well.[75]

Plantinga's main contention with this argument centres around the second premise. Regarding this point, he states that 'it is fair to say that it is step (2) – the assertion that existence in reality is greater than existence in the understanding alone – that is the troublemaker here'.[76] But is the idea of 'greatness' open to analysis? Leibniz thought not, arguing that it is 'impossible to demonstrate that perfections are incompatible – and he concluded from this that all perfections can co-exist together in a single entity'.[77] Plantinga, however, attempts to restate the argument, and does so in the following way:

(9) God does not exist in the actual world.

(10) For any worlds W and W' and object x, if x exists in W and x does not exist in W', then the greatness of x in W exceeds the greatness of x in

---

[75] Ibid, p. 199.
[76] Ibid.
[77] *Cosmological Argument*. [online]:
https://plato.stanford.edu/entries/cosmological-argument/.

W'.

(11) It is possible that God exists.

(12) So, there is a possible world W such that God exists in W according to (11).

(13) God exists in W and God does not exist in the actual world according to (9) and (12).

(14) If God exists in W and God does not exist in the actual world, it follows from (10) that the greatness of God in W exceeds the greatness of God in the actual world.

(15) Therefore, the greatness of God in W exceeds the greatness of God in the actual world according to (13) and (14).

(16) Accordingly, there is a possible being x and a world W such that the greatness of x in W exceeds the greatness of God in actuality (15).

(17) Thus, it is possible that there is a being greater than God is (16).

(18) Hence, it is possible that there could be a being greater than the being about which it is not possible to be greater than [from (17), by definition of 'God'].[78]

Moving from possibility to necessity in S5 (modal logic) is not contentious. This is because according to the rules of modal logic, if a particular proposition P is possible in some possible worlds, P entails Q; as Q is modally closed (either possible, necessary, or impossible), then the truth of Q is established.[79] It

---

[78] *The nature of necessity*. Clarendon Press, p. 199.
[79] Wingard, J. (1993). On a not quite yet "victorious" modal version of the ontological argument for the existence of God. *International Journal for Philosophy of Religion*, *33*(1), p. 56.

should be noted at this point that reference to 'possible worlds' is used heuristically in S5, even by modal anti-realists. This ultimately means that the relevance of such 'possible worlds' to 'reality' (however conceived) is irrelevant to the validity of the argument. Having said this, using S5 to make arguments from a possible necessity to a necessary necessity will open one up to 'parody arguments' which require additional debate about the soundness of the premises if the argument is to be sustained. Joshua Rasmussen and Alexander Pruss give the following parody example, where '@' refers to the 'actual world':[80]

> Negative Possibility.
>
> Possibly, there are no necessary beings. Given S5, it follows that:
>
> (40) There is no necessary being.
>
> Here is why. Suppose n is a necessary being in @. Then *n* will exist, and necessarily so, in every possible world by S4. And by S5, at every possible world *n* will be possibly a cause, and so n will be a necessary being. It follows, therefore, that if there actually is a necessary being, there necessarily is one. Hence if there possibly is no necessary being, then there is actually no necessary being.[81]

Rasmussen and Pruss go on to state that in order for the 'positive necessity' to be argued against 'negative necessity', one must '[invoke] some idea that positive states of affairs are more conceivable than negative ones'.[82]

---

[80] Rasmussen, J., & Pruss, A. (2018). *Necessary existence*. Oxford University Press (eBook), p. 29.
[81] Ibid, p. 31.
[82] Ibid.

Gödel's Ontological Argument

Having said this, Kurt Gödel's ontological proof resolves many of the issues here. Gödel's argument depends on two axioms: the first, stipulating that if a property is positive, then not a ($\sim$ A) is not positive. The second is that if A is positive, and A entails B, then B is positive.[83] What Godel means by 'positive' has been a subject of scholarly contention, with some[84] preferring to critique the argument by interpreting positivity in the 'moral/aesthetic' sense, despite admitting that it may simply mean 'attribution'. Such an interpretation leads Gustafsson (who references the two axioms stated above in S5) to state that 'being God-like seems positive and being Devil-like seems negative'.[85] But if one assumes – as Rasmussen and Pruss contend – that 'existing necessarily' is positive and possibly causing something is possible, then the ontological argument is certainly sustainable. Rasmussen and Pruss make the argument in a reductio format in the following way:

> To see this, for a reductio suppose A & B is impossible. Then nothing can have both A and B, and so necessarily anything that has A lacks B. Thus, A entails $\sim$ B. Hence $\sim$ B is positive by (2) since A is positive. By (1), B cannot be positive – and we have a contradiction. It follows from (3), (4), and (5) that N & C is possibly instantiated.[86]

(2) referred to above is effectively the assumption of *modus ponens*; (1) is Gödel's assumption that if A is positive, then not A is not positive. (3) is the assumption that existing

---

[83] *Necessary existence*, p. 151.
[84] Gustafsson, J. (2020). A patch to the possibility part of Godel's ontological proof. *The Analysis Trust, 80*(2), p. 230.
[85] Ibid, p. 233.
[86] *Necessary existence*, p. 151.

necessarily is positive, and (4) assumes that possibly causing something is positive. Though Gödel's argument is definitely valid in modal logic, assumptions such as the ones articulated by Pruss and Rasmussen are almost certainly susceptible to attack. Furthermore, the argument is virtually inaccessible to lay audiences when delivered in this way. That Kurt Gödel even attempted such an argument – and succeeded in securing its validity – is alone worthy of mention, as it dispels common New Atheistic notions of irrational or unprovable faith. Using such a long-winded argument that requires foreknowledge of modal logic, however, is not practical in pastoral or mainstream apologetic settings.

In this chapter we have been able to gauge the advantages and disadvantages of some ontological and cosmological arguments found in the Philosophy of Religion. We have issued comments on their practical utility from an apologetic perspective. With this in mind, the following conclusions can be made with reference to the *Kalām* cosmological argument, the main strength of using an argument like this is the brevity of its initial premises. The argument has generated much controversy and has been at the centre of the debates regarding God's existence. Having said this, the limitations of the argument relate to substantiating the second premise, especially when physics-based reasoning is referred to. Such reasoning has been highly volatile in the last century, and subsequently is less likely to meet the timeless criterion mentioned before. Arguing for a finite universe with a beginning is another contentious issue, as the argument demands that an actual infinity in the real world cannot exist. It is my estimation that the *Burhān* and *Tarkīb* arguments could be said to be more timeless and undercutting than the *Kalām* cosmological argument, as both the scientific reasoning needed for premise 2 of the latter and arguing against actual infinity are not requirements in order for the reasoning to be functional. This is especially relevant when considering infinite multiverse atheistic responses.

Relating to the ontological argument, the type of argument made by Plantinga can be said to be ineffectual in fulfilling the object of proving God's existence. As we have already seen, Plantinga actually admits this himself. The main disadvantage of this type of argument is the susceptibility of the formulations, which can ultimately lead to parody arguments that are just as valid and prove exactly the opposite of what is attempted. The way this issue is rectified is by proving a 'positive element' over a 'negative one', which requires an argument in and of itself. In my estimation, this is best done by Gödel. Having said this, the argument (while effective) is virtually inaccessible to lay audiences since it is written in S5 modal logic. Leibniz's argument (from a principle of sufficient reason) does not have the same type of limitations and may be used in its place instead. The *Burhān* argument works quite similarly to Leibniz's. But as we have seen, it has other features like the *Tarkīb* (composition) argument which strengthen the case for the contingency of the universe or multiverses.

In Application

Knowing Richard, he may reject the idea that the universe requires any sort of explanation at all. He may suggest that asking 'what is the explanation for the universe?' is an unnecessary question. We know however, that Richard doesn't apply this kind of logic to anything else in existence. If anything happens to Richard in his life which impacts it, he will demand some kind of an explanation. It is important to outline this to Richard, as Richard has one set of criteria in day-to-day living, but another set when dealing with the ultimate questions of life.

Chapter 4
PRESENTING THE ARGUMENTS

A range of arguments for God's existence that can and have been expressed in the realm of Philosophy of Religion have their roots in some of the medieval renditions covered in the previous chapters. Such arguments have made their way into the domain of popular debates, discussions, and articles. The importance of having the strongest possible theistic argument(s) cannot be overstated, as weak or overcomplicated arguments have less potency in any such conversations. In this chapter, I will present my arguments for God's existence, which find much of their inspiration from the *Burhān* argument. The arguments will aim to be both basic and effective in demonstrating the existence of a necessary existence. I will present five overall proofs, and then make two separate cosmological arguments in this context, with one from dependence and the other from causation. As for the ontological argument, I will present three possible formulations of it: the first will exclusively refer to dependence, the second to modal terms of contingency and necessity, while the third will argue from causation. To establish the will of the necessary being, I will use the argument of particularisation mentioned before. Finally, I will present a fine-tuning argument inspired by the *Burhān*. I will also offer three arguments for the oneness of the necessary existence to establish theistic monotheism. All these arguments should be understood in conjunction with each other to appreciate the veracity of the case being made. I will present the arguments formally. However they will be written in an accessible way intended for use by religious spokespeople to lay audiences.

Following Ibn Taymiyyah's distinction that prevents conflations between 'parts' and 'attributes', the word 'piece' will be used to mean something that 'can be removed, added, broken off, torn off or cut off from something'.[87] Furthermore, I distinguish between the terms 'causality' and 'dependence,' as an object can be caused by something but not be dependent on it to exist (i.e. a child in relation to his parents). However, the latter term entails that an object relies upon something for its continued existence.

Proof 1

Part I:

Proposition: There cannot be a world with only dependent thing(s) without reference to an independent thing, as dependent thing(s) cannot continue existing on their own. Existence is only explicable with reference to an independent existence, as impossible existences do not exist by logical necessity. Furthermore, dependent existences cannot self-generate or self-maintain.

Part II:

1. Everything made up of pieces is dependent.

2. The universe is made up of pieces.

3. Therefore, the universe is dependent.

Put in another way:

1. Everything made up of pieces is dependent.

---

[87] Collins. (n.d.). Definition of Piece [online]. Available at: https://www.collinsdictionary.com/dictionary/english/piece#:~:text=noun-,1.,when%20broken%20off%20or%20separated.

2. An infinite multiverse is made up of pieces.

3. Therefore, an infinite multiverse is dependent.

Expressed ontologically, the argument runs as follows:

Part I:

1. Any set with more than one member is dependent on its members.

2. An infinite set is a set with more than one member.

3. Therefore, an infinite set is dependent on its members.

The mathematical element of this argument helps safeguard the cosmological argument from the fallacy of composition, which states that what is true for the part must also be true of the whole. This is because it shows that the mereological distinctions of part/whole and dependence can be reasoned on *a priori* grounds, as well as cosmological ones. Having explained the distinction between a cause and dependency, at this point one may ask what is the distinction between dependence and independence on the one hand, and contingency and necessity on the other? Simply put, necessary things do not have to be independent. This is especially clear in the case of 'scientific necessities'. For example, consider the statement, 'Human beings cannot sprint 100 meters in one second.' This type of necessity does not need to be true in all possible worlds, universes, or conceptions, although it is true in our own.

Interestingly, a miracle could be defined as something that breaks scientific necessities, but not logical ones. Notwithstanding, the case for a differentiation in 'independence' and 'necessity' is made easier with so-called 'scientific necessities' – but what of logical ones? The argument being expressed here is that the category of necessary facts (like $2 + 2 = 4$) presupposes existence. This is because the most foundational thing conceivable is that 'there is no doubt that there is existence'. The category of existence is more basic than the category of facts; facts need to exist, but existence does not rely on anything. Thus, this may be said in the following manner:

Proof 2

Part I

1. Existence is presupposed in everything that is real.

2. Necessary facts are real.

3. Therefore, necessary facts presuppose existence.

Part II

1. If necessary facts presuppose existence, they depend on it.

2. Necessary facts presuppose existence.

3. Therefore, necessary facts depend on existence.

When I use the term 'independent', I mean self-sufficient. That is to say that which is independent does not need anything outside of it to explain or cause it. Nor does it have to depend on anything for its existence. As we have previously shown, not all necessary things are independent, as they rely on presupposed states of affairs in order to exist. Consequently, independence is more specific than necessity. Something which is independent must be necessary, but not all necessary things are independent. If this is true, then the argument of dependence above should bring about a critical reflection which concludes with an independent entity. This is because all things in the world have pieces, and all ontological composites depend on their members. To explain anything, we therefore need an independent entity upon which all other things depend, while it itself depends on nothing. This independent being will be necessary by definition, as anything 'independent' is necessary. If this is true, then it cannot be conceived of in any other way. If something cannot be conceived of in any other way, it must be so in all times and places, or independent of time and place. In both events it will be eternal. Eternality is thus not conceived as a 'positive quality' insomuch as it describes a lack of beginning or end. This shifts the burden of proof onto the interlocutor. They must either prove that eternality should be conceived in the ways I have described, or that it is possible for something immaterially necessary to possess the quality of beginning.

Making the argument using modal terms, I state:

1. Anything that can be conceivably rearranged abstractly is contingent.

2. The universe can be conceivably rearranged abstractly.

3. Therefore, the universe is contingent.

This can be expressed in another way:

1. Anything that can be conceivably rearranged abstractly is contingent.

2. An infinite multiverse can be conceivably rearranged abstractly.

3. Therefore, an infinite multiverse is contingent.

It is important to note here that I am not referencing causal contingency at this point. The argument can be made in the following mathematical or ontological way:

1. Any set that can be conceivably rearranged is contingent.

2. An infinite set can be conceivably rearranged.

3. Therefore, an infinite set is contingent.

Put simply, a set may have three members: A, B, and C. Such a set may be expressed as A, B, and C; B, C, and A; C, A, and B, and so on. This is the same set with a different arrangement. There is nothing necessary about this set being expressed as A, B, and C, as there is nothing which prevents one from changing the set by adding D or removing C. Thus, the set A, B, and C can be conceivably rearranged. The reason for mentioning 'abstractly' in this context is to circumvent the deterministic objection that all things are necessary because of an uninterrupted line of causal events. Ironically, some atheists may deny or doubt causality when confronted with the cosmological argument, yet they affirm it when making a case for determinism. Indeed, it is important in the field to look out for the interlocutor's metaphysical inconsistencies. Thus, the determinist may only make a claim for necessity as it relates to a specific object's connection with a God, an uninterrupted causal chain, or another similar substitute. Connected to this argument is the argument of particularisation, which establishes a will for the necessary existence. It runs as follows:

Proof 3

1. Anything that could be conceived of otherwise in abstraction was arranged by something else.

2. The universe could be conceived of otherwise in abstraction.

3. Therefore, the universe was arranged by something else.

Put in another way:

1. Anything that could be conceived otherwise in abstraction was arranged by something else.

2. An infinite multiverse could be conceived otherwise in

abstraction.

3. Therefore, an infinite multiverse was arranged by something else.

Following Proof 1 mentioned above, the 'something else' responsible for arranging the contingent thing must ultimately terminate in an independent/necessary 'something else'. The fact that an independent/necessary existence is capable of doing this would suggest the capacity to make choices. To arrange the universe/multiverse in one way rather than another indicates a choice; it chose that it should be one way rather than another. A question may be asked: is not the choice making capacity or 'will' of the independent existence itself something which can be conceived otherwise in abstraction? If so, would not the same problem with a universe or the multiverse be applicable to the independent existence? The fact that the independent existence is necessary means that all ways of describing the independent existence will also be necessary. That is to say that any attribute of the necessary existence, including 'will', is necessary. Therefore, if we establish that everything about the necessary existence is necessary, we also establish that nothing about the necessary existence is or can be contingent.

To bolster this opinion, one can make use of a variation of the fine-tuning argument, using necessity and contingency as a starting point.

Proof 4

1. The universe is fine-tuned for life by necessity or contingency.

2. If it is fine-tuned by necessity, then a necessary existence must account for the necessary fact of fine tuning.

3. If it is fine-tuned by contingency, then a necessary existence must account for any series of contingencies.

4. The universe is fine-tuned for life.

5. Therefore, the universe is fine-tuned for life by a necessary existence.

Premise 3 mentioned above links to the initial postulation, which states that there cannot exist only dependent existences as 'dependent thing(s) cannot continue existing on their own. Existence is only explicable with reference to an independent existence, as impossible existences do not exist by logical necessity and dependent existences cannot self-generate and or self-maintain'. Since contingency – like dependence – is something which is susceptible to generation, destruction, and could be arranged otherwise, the same thing can be said about an infinite series of 'dependent things' can likewise be said of an infinite series of contingent things. Notice the lack of mention of the terms 'chance' or 'randomness', which are usually employed in such arguments. These terms are themselves in need of justification by the atheist interlocutor, since they must prove that such a thing as 'chance' or 'randomness' exists, and that it is not merely an expression of one's ignorance of the mechanics of the universe or any other aspect of existence. Determinist atheists cannot in fact believe in 'chance' or 'randomness,' as concepts like these imply volatility and unpredictability – both of which are impossible in the deterministic worldview. Likewise, many compatibilist atheists would also agree with determinists on the predictable nature of the world.

The biggest weakness of fine-tuning arguments is the proponents use of scientific data (e.g. of the constants) to make their case. To circumvent this objection, one may reference regularity, stability, and uniformity of nature (which are presuppositions of scientific work) as better starting points than the fine-tuning of constants. On this point, John Haldane states:

> Stability, regularity, and intelligibility in world and mind are underlying assumptions of even the most limited claims of scientific realism. But suppose we ask what reason we have for making these assumptions. The general answer cannot be that they are *conclusions* of scientific enquiry, since they are part of what makes it possible.[88]

That water would boil at 100 degrees today, yesterday, and tomorrow is an assumption of scientists when measuring the temperature of water. It is not due to repeated investigation of water temperature for every day and in every environment. If it were even possible that water could boil 100 degrees today, -100 tomorrow, and 1,000 the next day, scientific research would be fruitless. This, of course, also applies to quantum mechanics, which additionally requires axioms and assumptions to work. That the universe is complicated (consisting of many pieces), stable, and mechanistic is evidence that the necessary existence (which preponderated it) has knowledge. Having said this, an argument for uniformity could be stated in the following way:

Part I

1. The fact of the universe being uniform, regular, and stable must be either contingent or necessary.

2. If it is necessary, then a necessary existence must account for it.

3. If it is contingent, a necessary existence must also account for it.

---

[88] Smart, J J C and Haldane, John (2001). *Atheism and theism*. Oxford: Blackwell Publishing, p. 83.

4. The universe is uniform, regular, and stable.

5. Therefore, a necessary existence accounts for it.

Part II

Assuming that uniformity, stability, and regularity are necessary facts of the universe, one may argue *reductio* by stating:

1. A contingent existence cannot sufficiently account for the necessary fact of the regularity, stability, and uniformity of the universe.

2. The universe is a contingent existence.

3. Therefore, the universe cannot sufficiently account for the necessary fact of the regularity, stability, and uniformity of the universe.

Proof 5

The arguments one may employ do not need to have the inception of the world (or universe) as one of their premises. This is not because an eternal universe cannot be successfully refuted, but only to undermine the argument of the interlocutor. The argument may run as follows:

1. Anything made up of pieces is caused.

2. The universe is made up of pieces.

3. Therefore, the universe is caused.

Or, put in another way:

1. Anything made up of pieces is caused.

2. An infinite multiverse is made up of pieces.

3. Therefore, an infinite multiverse is caused.

With these five proofs, one should be able to competently

make a case against atheism. In addition, it should be outlined on the field that atheism has no explanatory scope to answer the most fundamental questions, let alone explain 'all that exists'. Atheism itself lacks any explanatory or refutational scope.

After proving that a necessary existence exists, it is befitting for those intending to establish the validity of monotheistic theism to offer three additional arguments for the oneness of such a necessary existence. These arguments take their inspiration from the *Burhān* and *Dalīl al Tamanu'*, including viewpoints presented by Muslim thinkers like al-Ghazālī in his book *Al-Iqtiṣād fi al 'Itiqād*.

Argument 1

1. If a necessary existence is an existence that cannot be any other way, there cannot be more than one.

2. A necessary existence cannot be any other way.

3. Therefore, there cannot be more than one necessary existence.

If there was anything to demarcate 'necessary existence 1' from 'necessary existence 2,' that property of demarcation would disqualify 'necessary existence 2' from being necessary, by definition. This is because it would be conceived that 'necessary existence 2' could be 'another way' and therefore 'necessary existence 2' would not be necessary at all in this case. Instead, it would be considered contingent. For instance, if one supposes God 1 is necessary in all aspects and God 2 is different from God 1, that which differentiates God 2 from God 1 will indicate contingency in at least one of the 'Gods', or even both. If power is a necessary attribute of God 1 – and God 1 is necessarily powerful – but 'God 2' does not exhibit power by necessity, then this means that God 2 does not meet the criterion of necessity required to be the 'necessary existence'.

Argument 2

Part I

1. If the necessary existence is responsible for all other things in existence, then the necessary existence has capacity over all things in existence.

2. The necessary existence is responsible for all other things in existence.

3. Therefore, the necessary existence has capacity over all things in existence.

Part II

1. If the necessary existence has ultimate capacity over all things in existence, nothing other than the necessary existence is over all things capable.

2. The necessary existence has capacity over all things in existence.

3. Therefore, the necessary existence is over all things capable.

Argument 3

1. For nature to be stable, uniform, and regular, there must only be one external agent arranging the world.

2. Nature is stable, uniform, and regular.

3. Therefore, there must be only one external agent arranging the world

It could be argued that a collection of 'minds' cooperated together to allow nature to be stable, uniform and regular.

However, if the one who is all capable is responsible for the existence of such minds, then they will also be responsible for whatever such minds produce.

The collection of proofs and arguments I have provided above establishes the necessity, choice making capability, ultimate capacity, independence, and oneness of the necessary existence. As initially stated, a necessary existence must exist to account for the continued existence of the world. Furthermore, a necessary existence must exist to account for any existence whatsoever, as 'dependent existences' could neither generate nor maintain themselves. To make these arguments effective in pastoral and apologetic settings, one should start by asking fundamental thought-provoking questions, such as, 'Why is there something rather than nothing?' This question – despite its simplicity – is profound enough to engender deep thoughts and strike existential chords within the recipient, drawing the interlocutor towards theism in a manner more valuable than argumentation.

In terms of analogies and metaphors, Joshua Rasmussen (who authored a book specifically for lay audiences) gives the example of a stack of bricks on the ground, in which the stack of bricks represents dependent things, and the floor represents the independent entity.[89] One may also use the example of the sea floor and the sea, and how one assumes the dependence of the water's settlement without visualising the sea floor. This brings to mind just how clear the case for independence is. To young people (who may be familiar with their smartphones), one may give the example of the mobile phone depending on charge, with the charge depending on some sort of power plant. Without any exception, this process terminates with a self-sufficient independent entity.

---

[89] Rasmussen, J. (2019). *How reason can lead to God.* InterVarsity Press, p. 4.

Likewise, when referencing causation, one can argue that anything which is composed of pieces is causally contingent. I am made up of my body parts, a fact which indicates that I was pieced together by something external to me. The universe is made up of many pieces, which denotes that something external to it pieced it together as well. Imagery is important in these arguments if they are to be effective before laypeople, as is questioning and placing the burden of proof on the atheist interlocutor. Worthwhile questions in this regard include: Can existence be explained by non-existence? What is nonexistence, and is it even conceivable without reference to existence? Is zero ever intelligible without reference to natural and negative numbers? Can there be a state of affairs where only dependent things depend upon dependent things *ad infinitum*? How do you justify such a state of affairs cosmologically or on *a priori* grounds? Questions like these are important to show the power of the theistic position, as well as the utterly impotent nature of the opposing view.

In Application

Much of the New Atheist polemic against religion depends on notions which imply that religion is 'outdated'. Both Richard and Betty seem affected by this kind of discourse. The simple fact that educated scientists and other kinds of intellectuals choose to be atheists can be influential in keeping someone from positively engaging with theism. Richard and Betty are both fascinated with Bertrand Russell for example. They may even quote him directly when making a case against theism. On strictly logical terms, this is obviously inconsequential and an 'appeal to authority'. Both Richard and Betty are clever enough to know that. Psychologically, as shown in multiple studies (most notably Milgram's Shock Experiment), one cannot be sure that Richard and Betty are not immune influenced by the intellectual status of some atheists like Russell. It may be a simple, yet powerful, point of reminder therefore to simply outline the sheer number of intellectual contributors who not only were theists, but argued for theism throughout the years.

Chapter 5
OBJECTIONS

This chapter will deal with the most common objections to the various articulations of the cosmological and ontological arguments that have been formulated. Some of them are not directly relevant to my proofs and arguments mentioned in the previous chapter, nevertheless I will actively demonstrate why this is the case. Other objections are more relevant to my formulation of the argument, however, and will thus be dealt with more systematically. In addition to outlining these objections, I will outline how they should be dealt with technically and rhetorically by those contending with them in pastoral and apologetic contexts, as delivery can sometimes be of greater importance than content.

First, affirming or denying the initial proposition made in the previous chapter ultimately leads to capitulation:

> Proposition: There cannot be a world with only dependent thing(s) without reference to an independent thing, as a dependent thing(s) cannot continue existing on their own. Existence is only explicable with reference to an independent existence. This is because impossible existences do not exist by logical necessity, and dependent existences cannot self-generate and/or self-maintain.

The interlocutor may deny this statement, claiming that there can be a world with only dependent things that can continue to exist, generate, or maintain themselves. With such a claim, the interlocutor will effectively be affirming that such existences collectively are independent, which effectively means that they have in fact capitulated. If the interlocutor agrees with the proposition above, then no further argument is necessary. Unfortunately, for the interlocutor the dependent/independent dichotomy is exhaustive, which means a third option cannot be produced. If the initial capitulation is made, subsequent arguments of composition will then be levelled at the interlocutor.

Objection 1: The fallacy of composition

Since the fallacy of composition suggests that a false generalisation has been made from part to whole, it is perhaps important for us to start by outlining different types of 'parts' in the study of mereology. Parts may be 'attached', 'detached', 'cognitively or functionally salient', 'arbitrarily demarcated', 'self-connected', 'homogenous', 'gerrymandered', 'material', 'immaterial', 'extended' or 'un-extended', or 'spatial' or 'temporal'.[90] When I use the term 'part' I do so in compliance with the common usage of the term 'piece' in the English language, which specifically deals with 'attached' and 'detached' categories of parthood.

In his famous debate with Copleston, Bertrand Russell famously stated that 'every man who exists has a mother, and it seems to me your argument is that therefore the human race must have a mother'.[91] Applying this reasoning to the *Kalām* cosmological argument, this would translate to a statement like, 'We see causes in the universe, so there must be a cause

---

[90] Varzi, W. (2003). Mereology [online]. Accessible at: https://plato.stanford.edu/entries/mereology/.
[91] Allen, D. (1989). *Christian belief in a post-modern world.* John Knox Press, p. 6.

of the universe.' This is analogous to stating that since the parts of a whale are small, the whale itself must be small. Naturally, this is not necessarily the case, as the part/whole distinction does not need to be disparate. Both the individual pearls in the pearl necklace may be white, as well as the entire necklace. To claim (with certainty) that one is committing a 'fallacy of composition' (or that one is not), one must have complete knowledge of both the parts and whole of an object to analyse whether the correspondence between the parts and the whole is disparate or not. This has been the standard way of responding to this kind of contention. However, there are other more effective methods regarding the arguments made in the previous chapter that we can employ instead.

As has been shown, the case for dependency can be made both ontologically (on *a priori* mathematical grounds) and cosmologically. The postulation that something made of pieces is dependent on those pieces for its existence is not a generalisation from part to whole, but a direct definitional claim about the whole. A whole with pieces is the sum of its parts, and the whole would not be as it is without its pieces. If a Gucci pearl necklace is made up of 10 pearl pieces and I replace 3 such pieces with plastic pearls, it is no longer a Gucci pearl necklace. It is now just an imitation of it. If I replace the wheels and engine of a Lamborghini Murcielago with some other wheels and engine, I no longer have the right to call this car a Lamborghini Murcielago. Of course, in everyday examples one may talk of socially acceptable removals and additions, such that if I remove one single bolt from the Lamborghini, it will still maintain its status as a Lamborghini. But on strictly material grounds, it would be impossible to state that it is the same Lamborghini as it was, without redefining what a Lamborghini is. Thus, our definition of the car depends on our understanding of what makes it what it is.

Applying this idea to the universe, if we assume that the universe is expanding, then with every passing second, we are confronted with a new kind of universe. Even if we assume that the universe is eternal or static, and we conceive of removing all the pieces of the universe from it to the point where the universe no longer exists, then we have proven that the universe is contingent and dependent. If it were possible for me to destroy your mobile phone or make it change its state to a point of indistinguishability, then I have proven that your mobile phone is not necessary. One may ask that if this is the case, and a human being is made up of his constituent body parts, then assuming that all his bodily cells are replaced, will we be talking about another human being altogether? On strictly materialistic grounds the answer is yes; it is really only religious and philosophical discourses that encourage us to define human beings by the immaterial soul.

Moreover, the universe can be conceived of in another way that does not break logical necessities, which further proves its contingency. Anything that can be conceived of in another way in abstraction is contingent; the universe can be conceived of in another way in abstraction, which therefore means that the universe is contingent. An objection may be to say: The necessary existence can be conceived of as creating and not creating the universe. Therefore, the necessary existence is contingent, but (as mentioned in the previous chapter) if necessity characterises every aspect of the necessary existence, it also characterises the necessary existence's will. Since creation or non-creation is directed by the necessary existence's will, it may be said that the existence of the universe is necessarily instantiated through the necessary existence. An atheist determinist may object that nothing is contingent since it has been determined by an uninterrupted line of causal events. In reference to determinism this is true, but this is only true by virtue of this connection. On the other hand, it is not true if we isolate the variables of the object or thing in question. For the atheistic interlocutor to prove otherwise, they must show how it is possible that any said object or thing (which could have been conceived otherwise) cannot be so without reference to the causal chain. Such an interlocutor is not required to show that this is the case, but only that it could conceivably be the case in absolute abstraction, which is impossible. This example illustrates how those espousing the theistic position in the field cannot afford to dread questioning the questioner, as doing so will give the atheistic questioner false confidence.

Admittedly, the objection has some force with the *Kalām* argument and arguments like it that explicitly rely on induction in establishing the first premise. For one to make a general claim from a limited sample, there is the secondary issue of the problem of induction (especially considering quantum mechanics), which may weaken these types of arguments.

The most that can be said is that Russell's objection will force the theist who uses the *Kalām* argument into a gridlock of ignorance, since both the atheist and the theist have ignorance of the correspondence (or lack thereof) between the whole and its part. As we have seen, this is not relevant to the Burhān inspired argument put forward in the previous chapter.

Objection 2: An infinite universe

The *Burhān* argument shows how an infinite regress is not a necessary existence. It does so by not arguing that infinity is mathematically or actually impossible, but through composition (*tarkīb*) instead. Even if one assumed the validity of an infinite multiverse, it would not affect the argument at all, since a multiverse is a) dependent on its pieces, and b) able to be conceived of in another way in abstraction. Therefore, this objection, though relevant to some forms of the cosmological argument, has no bearing at all to the *Burhān.*

Objection 3: 'The universe just is'

Bertrand Russell may as well have said 'the universe is the universe' or 'the universe exists'. It reminds me of when I reprimand my three-year old daughter and ask her why she has misbehaved. In such cases, she simply replies 'because', while offering no explanation whatsoever. This causes one to wonder why Russell does not apply the same reasoning to other things in existence, instead of simply peculiarising the universe in this way. Richard Swinburne (in a more than satisfactory refutation of this line of reasoning) states:

> The objection fails to make any crucial distinction between the universe and other objects; and so it fails in its attempt to prevent at the outset a rational inquiry into the issue of whether the universe has some origin outside itself.[92]

Objection 4: Causal scepticism and retro-causality

A vernacular dictionary definition of causation is something which produces an effect. A more formal definition runs as follows: 'C is a cause of E if, and only if, C and E are actual and C, *ceteris paribus,* is sufficient for E'.[93] A cause does not need to be one directional, or indeed bound by time at all; only some conceptions of causation are envisioned like this. John Mackie refers to this specific type of causality as 'causal priority'.[94] On the issue of directionality, John Mackie states

---

[92] Swinburne, R. (2004). *The existence of God.* Oxford University Press, pp. 134-135.
[93] Tooley and Sosa. (2011). *Causation.* Oxford: Oxford University Press, p. 5.

that 'it is conceivable that there should be evidence for backwards causation, with A being causally prior to P and P temporally prior to A'.[95] These conceptions of retro causality require additional evidence. As Karl Popper states, 'If a stone dropped into a pool, the entry of the stone will explain the expanding circular waves. This would demand a vast number of distant coherent generators of waves – the coherence of which, to be explicable, would have to be shown as operating from one centre'.[96] The possibility of this proposition (or the lack thereof) depends on one's conception of the direction of time.

William Craig dedicates much of his argumentative effort into arguing against a static theory of time. Since the arguments presented in the previous chapter relating to causation did not have a time element, the issues of backward causation are irrelevant for the analysis articulated here. It must be also remembered that any cause-based objection will only be relevant to the last of the five proofs mentioned in the previous chapter, as the first four do not rely on causation.

Though causal scepticism (or even causal nihilism) does not pose a threat to our arguments, one must also highlight the implications of taking this objection seriously without a reasonable metaphysical substitute. For one then must call into serious question the scientific method itself, as it 'can hardly be denied that such knowledge is indispensable in science'.[97] Like regularity, causality is presupposed by science, not discoverable by it. Pastorally, if one is discussing the issue with an atheist, it is likely that they believe in Darwinian

---

[94] Mackie, J. (2011). Causes and conditions in *causation*. Oxford University Press, p. 50.
[95] Ibid.
[96] Popper, Karl R. (1956) *The Arrow of Time*. Nature 177, p. 538.
[97] Mackie, J. (2011). *Causes and conditions in causation*. Oxford University Press, p. 52.

evolution. Scientific theories like evolution require causality, and so an atheist who is committed to evolutionary theory cannot be a causal sceptic.

Objection 5: Something from nothing

Nothing can be defined as the absence of something. New Atheist Lawrence Krauss wrote a book entitled *A Universe from Nothing*. In this work, he uses the term 'nothing' as interchangeable with 'empty space'. In an important passage of his work, he states:

> To summarize then: the observation that the universe is flat and that the local Newtonian gravitational energy is essentially zero today strongly suggests that our universe arose through a process of inflation, a process whereby the energy of empty space (nothing) gets converted into energy of something, during a time when the universe is driven closer and closer to being essentially exactly flat on all observable scales.[98]

In the following pages, Krauss essentially refutes his own earlier comment by stating:

> While inflation demonstrates how empty space endowed with energy can effectively create everything we see, along with an unbelievably large and flat universe, it would be disingenuous to suggest that empty space endowed with energy, which drives inflation, is really nothing. In this picture, one must assume that space exists and can store energy…so if we stop here, one might be justified in claiming that modern science is a long way from really addressing

---

[98] Krauss, L. (2012). *A universe from nothing*. New York: Free Press, p. 75.

how to get something from nothing. This is just the first step, however. As we expand our understanding, we will next see that inflation can represent simply the tip of a cosmic iceberg of nothingness.[99]

This assertion is essentially self-refuting. In a famous debate between Krauss and Hamza Tzortzis in 2012 which garnered over four million views, Krauss was asked why he named chapter 9 of his book 'Nothing is Something'. To this question Krauss responded with the following answer: 'I like catchy phrases, and when I said nothing is something, it's a chapter title'.[100] As we have seen, the strongest types of 'nothing' arguments have been delivered in a modal language and refer to conceivability. This was in fact the argument of David Hume. It is the very same modal language that can establish 'positivity' or 'necessity' over 'non-existence' and 'negativity' (refer to the discussion of Gödel's ontological argument in the previous chapter). Since the existence of the former in some possible worlds overrides the non-existence of the latter, it follows that the existence of the latter is established.

These objections are by no means exhaustive. As alluded to in the previous chapter, there are individuals who, like Quine, are sceptical of the modal categories, while others reject any kind of ontological reasoning whatsoever. It is beyond the scope of this book to have a full exposition of these points in this section and decisively deal with each objection in considerable depth. This chapter's purpose was to address the most relevant objections expressed against the arguments

---

[99] Ibid.
[100] Islamic Education and Research Academy. (2013, March 29). *Islam vs Atheism. Hamza Tzortzis vs Lawrence Krauss*. [online]. Available at: https://www.youtube.com/watch?v=uSwJuOPG4FI& (1:43).

provided in the previous chapter. In practical application, one must discern the atheist's epistemological starting point to subsequently offer them the most effective arguments that are least vulnerable to attack. In this way, one can ultimately choose to start with an ontological or cosmological argument, and a cause based or a dependency-based argument. All of this depends on the identity of the interlocutor.

In application

The kind of objections I tackle in this chapter are the most common ones I have encountered in the field. I have mentioned the top-5 for the sake of brevity and conciseness not because other more sophisticated renditions of the *Burhan* (or arguments I have presented) do not exist. Having said this, based on my experience in the field, the likelihood that an interlocutor will use one of the five objections (or a combination of more than one of them) is high. On the point of retro-causality, Richard may use quantum mechanics to cast aspersions on the process and function of causation. He may argue, using the grandfather paradox for example, that future causes can create prior effects. The grandfather paradox states that if a grandson goes back in time and kills his grandfather, this should make his own existence impossible. Applying this to the universe, Richard may want to argue that the universe may have caused itself. One can argue that this kind of thing is impossible on logical grounds just as in the case of a mother giving birth to herself. Retro-causation, however, is not the same as retro-contingency or retro-dependence. The latter imply a perpetual reliance of the universe on itself. If Richard makes this point, one agrees that the universe is independent and self-sufficient, which is an untenable position as per the arguments presented in this book.

Betty may accept the arguments on face value and suggest that there is a necessary existence. 'What about the other religious attributes of God?' she may ask. 'What about love, mercy and forgiveness?'. It could be said that details of the divine attributes are understood through a religious text wherein God has revealed who he is to the world. Of course, Betty needs to be convinced that such text is inspired by God, but this goes beyond the scope of this book. It may be useful to engage Betty experientially, drawing upon her first-person subjective experiences. Love, for example, is inexplicable to most people but from whence did it come? Religious narratives would indicate that the source of love is the necessary existence itself. This is because an entity which is deplete of something cannot usually cause another entity to have a quality that it doesn't have. An explanation must be given, for example, for someone who wants to suggest that life can emerge from lifelessness.

CONCLUSION

In this book we covered some of the main arguments for God's existence, with a particular focus on contingency arguments. We carefully traced the history of these arguments and found that there is a staggering level of agreement among the greatest minds known to history on the effectiveness of such lines of reasoning. We devoted special attention to the *Burhān* argument formulated by Ibn Sīnā, which makes theologically and philosophically watertight arguments suitable for use in apologetic and pastoral settings. Throughout the book (and especially in chapter 5), we dealt with some of the main objections presented against the argument. We have demonstrated that virtually all these objections were in some way anticipated by the initial formulators of the argument. In addition, the book considered the so-called 'New Atheist' contributions to this discourse. It found that instead of providing any valuable contributions, many of these contemporary figures have only demonstrated misguided or lazy treatments of the subject matter. The failure to uncover what New Atheists say about the *Burhān* argument or its permutations – on the internet, in their most famous publications, or otherwise – is suggestive of the fact that such figures have never had to deal with this line of interrogation from a theist. With changing demographics and the growth of agnosticism, the stakes are too high to not introduce these types of arguments in the areas of apologetics and polemics. Considering current demographic trends, theology as a discipline itself may lose relevance (in the UK in particular), especially if the first premise of the discipline (namely, the existence of God) cannot be argued for in a proper way.

Having said this, we have seen through the hypothetical scenarios in each chapter that a cold and rational approach by itself can never be sufficient. For the atheist detractor to feel truly comfortable with the arguments presented, they will usually need to feel comfortable with the person making these arguments. Despite personally being unaware of any formal psychological studies conducted on this matter with clearly defined parameters, it is perhaps the case that past trauma and relationship difficulties can sometimes be a key indicator to the theological attitudes which people have. Ironically, sometimes the best way to convince someone of God is to refrain from arguing for God's existence. Sometimes arguments of detractors need to be attacked, but in other cases it takes bravery not to attack. Pastorally, one must read the prevailing mood and assess the available options. Being emotionally and socially intelligent can sometimes be more valuable than having the best arguments civilisation has had to offer.

Manufactured by Amazon.ca
Bolton, ON

25397644R00046